Sheet Pan Weeknight Meals For Two

65 Delicious Sheet Pan Supper Recipes
For Poultry, Pork, Beef & Other Meat,
Vegetable And Seafood Dishes

ALLISON BARNES

ISBN-13: 978-1516800452

ISBN-10: 1516800451

DEDICATION

To couples everywhere who are not too busy to cook delicious homemade meals.

TABLE OF CONTENT

Read Other Books By Allison Barnes:

Cast Iron Skillet Weeknight Meals For Two: 56 Delicious Cast Iron Skillet Recipes For Poultry, Pork, Beef & Other Meat, Vegetable And Seafood Dishes

INTRODUCTION

Sheet Pan Weeknight Meals For Two is a collection of 65 recipes for couples that will enable you to cook delicious and healthy meals without spending too much time in the kitchen. Most of the recipes can be prepared within 30 minutes while only a few require over an hour. Sheet pans are not just for baking cookies. They can be used to prepare a variety of delicious meals from oven "stir-fries" to pork chops and vegetables roasts.

Quick dinners don't get better than this – just crank up your oven, combine the ingredients on a sheet pan and voila!, dinner is ready. Cooking with a sheet pan enables you to get a lot done in a short time without any complicated procedure. Cooking dinner can be overwhelming after returning from a hectic day at work. This is why this book is filled with quick and easy recipes that do not have any complications.

Most cookbooks you will find provide the standard recipes for four or six servings and you have to start calculating how to cook for two. All the work has been done for you in the recipes in this book. Each one of them is made for two, so all you have to do is to follow the instructions to create a healthy dish for you and your partner. The nutritional information for each serving is also provided so you can know exactly what you are consuming.

Once you start a relationship with your first sheet pan, it is a love affair that will last a lifetime. Cooking for two is easy when you have a sheet pan. You have less to wash when you make one-dish meals. Sheet pans are very handy no matter the season. You can use them to roast vegetables and create full meals. Cooking with this appliance provides a simpler way of getting dinner on the table easily and quickly. Not only do they save time, they also enable you to create food that is rich in texture and wonderful in taste.

Although, many of the recipes in this book can be cooked in other types of baking dishes, it is advisable to invest in a sheet pan. You can get by with just two 13 by 18 inch "rimmed baking sheets or "half sheets". They are sturdy pans with 1-inch rims and they allow easy circulation of hot air when you are cooking. They will enable you to maximize the results of the recipes as well as the flavor of the dish.

If it has not been easy for you to get good meals on the table, your answer is here. Sheet pan meals will totally change your idea of cooking for two. You can easily adapt them to your specifications and cleaning is easy. The meals can be broiled, baked, or roasted for easy preparation. Some recipes require a rimmed sheet pan while you can use flat for others. Lining the pans with parchment paper or aluminum foil makes it easy to clean up after cooking sticky meals. You can also make a packet for you and your partner.

Read through each recipe and get everything ready before you start cooking. Trim fat from pork and beef. You are free to choose how to arrange items on the sheet but it is better to place thicker cuts of meat at the center of the pan and veggies on the outside for perfect cooking. Although a list of spices are provide for each recipe, you can interchange with your favorite spices. A little of this or that is all you need to transform a dish and come up with your own creation.

Chicken recipes can use breasts, thighs or tenders. Beef recipes can use sirloin, steak strips, flat iron steak, roast, ground beef or your choice of beef cut. Pork can use ham, sausage, pork chops, pork tenderloin or bacon. Fish has a wide arrange from shrimp, clams, scallops, mussels, tilapia, cod, catfish, grouper, lobster or tuna. Vegetables in these dishes can range from squash, potatoes, tomatoes, green beans, corn, onions, cilantro, etc. The choices are endless.

Most households have limited time to cook. That is why most of the recipes here have been chosen because they are quick to make. Cooking shouldn't be a chore. It is a gift that we can all enjoy. You will appreciate this recipes because they will help you to save time and also come up with meals that will be thoroughly satisfactory. Your search for inspired recipes for two is over. Get the sheet pan, foil and apron ready and let's get started!

Thank you for allowing me to share with you.

Allison Barnes

SHEET PAN POULTRY RECIPES FOR TWO

Chicken Breasts With Apple Glaze

This easy delicious entrée for two comes out beautifully browned, moist and flavorful.

Serves: 2

Preparation: 10 minutes

Total Time: 60 minutes

Ingredients:

2 bone-in, chicken breast halves

3 tablespoons reduced-sodium soy sauce

1/4 cup unsweetened apple juice

Directions:

1. Place chicken breasts in a rack on a sheet pan.

2. Combine soy sauce and apple juice and pour over chicken.

3. Bake, uncovered at 350°F for about 50-60 minutes. Baste with pan juices occasionally.

Nutritional Counter Per Serving:

Calories 355, Carbs 6.0g, Protein 42.0g, Fat 17.0g, Cholesterol 129mg, Sodium 445mg, Fiber 1.0g

Baked Chicken And Vegetables
Flavorful marinated chicken with veggies.

Serves: 2

Preparation: 20 minutes, plus marinating

Total Time: 60 minutes

Ingredients:

2 boneless, skinless chicken breast halves

2 teaspoons reduced-sodium soy sauce

1 tablespoon reduced-sodium teriyaki sauce

1 tablespoon Worcestershire sauce

1 tablespoon balsamic vinegar

1 tablespoon olive oil

2 large fresh mushrooms, sliced

1 small potato, peeled, cut into cubes

1 small green pepper, diced

1 large carrot, sliced

1/3 cup chopped onion

6 pitted ripe olives, halved

1/2 teaspoon Italian seasoning

1 tablespoon grated Parmesan cheese

Directions:

1.In a small bowl, mix together soy sauce, teriyaki sauce, Worcestershire sauce, balsamic vinegar and olive oil. Pour 2 tablespoons of the mixture into a resealable bag. Cover the remaining marinade and place in the fridge.

2. Add chicken breasts to the bag, seal and shake to coat. Place in the refrigerator for 3-4 hours.

3. Line sheet pan with foil and spray with cooking spray.

4. Drain marinade and discard. Place chicken in the sheet pan.

5. Spread mushrooms, potato, green pepper, carrot and olives around the chicken.

6. Drizzle with the remaining marinade then sprinkle with Italian seasoning and cheese.

7. Cover with foil and bake at 375°F for 40-45 minutes.

Nutritional Counter Per Serving:

Calories 337, Carbs 26.0g, Protein 33.0g, Fat 11.0g, Cholesterol 81.0mg, Sodium 576mg, Fiber 4.0g

Three-Ingredient Onion Chicken

Leftover french-fried onions can be used for other recipes.

Serves: 2

Preparation: 5 minutes

Total Time: 30 minutes

Ingredients:

2 chicken breast halves, boneless skinless

2 tablespoons of honey mustard

1/2 cup french-fried onions, crushed

Directions:

1. Line a sheet pan with foil.

2. Coat the chicken with honey mustard then roll in the french-fried onions.

3. Place on sheet pan and bake at 375°F for about 20-25 minutes.

Nutritional Counter Per Serving:

Calories 310, Carbs 15.0g, Protein 31.0g, Fat 14.0g, Cholesterol 79mg, Sodium 322mg, Fiber 1.0g

Chicken Cordon Bleu

An easy fix when you need fast dinner for the two of you.

Serves: 2

Preparation: 15 minutes

Total Time: 55 minutes

Ingredients:

2 chicken breast halves, boneless skinless

2 slices Swiss cheese

2 slices deli ham

1/2 cup dry bread crumbs

1/8 teaspoon paprika

1/2 teaspoon salt

1/4 cup butter, melted

Directions:

1. Place chicken between plastic wraps and use a mallet to flatten to about 1/4-inch thickness.

2. Top each breast with ham and cheese. Roll up chicken breasts, tuck in the ends and hold with toothpicks.

3. In a shallow bowl, mix together bread crumbs, paprika and salt. Place butter in another bowl.

4. Dip chicken in the butter then roll in the bread crumb mixture.

5. Coat a sheet pan with cooking spray, place the chicken on it and bake for 40-45 minutes at 350°F. Discard toothpicks and serve.

Nutritional Counter Per Serving:

Calories 441, Carbs 10.0g, Protein 46.0g, Fat 23.0g, Cholesterol 157mg, Sodium 788mg, Fiber 1.0g

Mozzarella Baked Chicken Breasts

A no-fuss, delicious entree.

Serves: 2

Preparation: 20 minutes

Total Time: 50 minutes

Ingredients:

2 chicken breast halves, boneless skinless

1/8 teaspoon pepper

1/2 cup reduced-sodium chicken broth, warmed

1-1/2 cups stuffing mix

2 tablespoons white wine

2/3 cup condensed cream of chicken soup

1 garlic clove, minced

2 slices part-skim mozzarella cheese, shredded

Directions:

1. Rub pepper all over the chicken. Coat a deep baking pan with cooking spray and place the chicken in it.

2. Combine broth and stuffing mix in a small bowl. Set aside for 3 minutes then spoon around the chicken.

3. Combine the wine, soup and garlic then spread the mixture over chicken. Add the mozzarella cheese.

4. Cover and bake for 25 minutes at 350°F. After 15 minutes, uncover and bake for 5-10 minutes more.

Nutritional Counter Per Serving:

Calories 471, Carbs 35.0g, Protein 42.0g, Fat 16.0g, Cholesterol 95mg, Sodium 1690mg, Fiber 1.0g

Chicken With Apricot Glaze

Serves: 2

Preparation: 5 minutes

Total Time: 30 minutes

Ingredients:

2 chicken breast halves, boneless skinless

1/4 cup apricot preserves

1/4 cup mayonnaise

2 tablespoons of dried minced onion

Directions:

1. Place chicken in a rimmed sheet pan.

2. Combine the other ingredients and spoon over the chicken.

3. Bake, uncovered for 25 minutes at 350°F.

Nutritional Counter Per Serving:

Calories 430, Carbs 29.0g, Protein 23.0g, Fat 25.0g, Cholesterol 73mg, Sodium 222mg, Fiber 1.0g

Chicken Breasts Stuffed With Asparagus And Cheese

Serves: 2

Preparation: 20 minutes

Total Time: 45 minutes

Ingredients:

2 large chicken breast halves, boneless, skinless

8 asparagus spears, trimmed, divided

1/4 cup Italian seasoned bread crumbs

1/2 cup shredded mozzarella cheese, divided

Salt to taste

Black pepper to taste

Directions:

1. Preheat the oven to 375°F. Grease a rimmed sheet pan.

2. Place chicken breasts between plastic wraps and use a mallet to flatten to about 1/4-inch thickness. Season with salt and pepper on each side.

3. Place 4 asparagus spears on each chicken breast and spread 1/4 cup of cheese over the asparagus.

4. Roll up each chicken breast and place seam side down on the greased pan. Sprinkle with the bread crumbs.

5. Bake for about 25 minutes.

Nutritional Counter Per Serving:

Calories 390, Carbs 13.4g, Protein 57.5g, Fat 10.8g, Cholesterol 147mg, Sodium 581mg, Fiber 1.8g

Couple's Night Turkey Meat Loaf
Juicy and tender meatloaf.

Serves: 2

Preparation: 10 minutes

Total Time: 70 minutes

Ingredients:

1/2 pound ground turkey

1 cup cubed bread

1 1/2 teaspoons teriyaki sauce

4 1/2 teaspoons water

1 egg, beaten

1 tablespoon chopped green pepper

2 tablespoons chopped onion

1 tablespoon shredded cheddar cheese

1 tablespoon shredded mozzarella cheese

Dash celery seed

Dash garlic powder

1 tablespoon grated Parmesan cheese

Directions:

1. In a bowl, mix together bread cubes, teriyaki sauce and water. Set aside for 5 minutes.

2. Add the turkey, egg, green pepper, onion, cheddar, mozzarella, celery seed and garlic powder. Mix well with your hands.

3. Place parchment on rimmed sheet pan. Place the turkey mixture on the sheet pan and shape it into a loaf. Sprinkle with the Parmesan cheese.

4. Place in the oven and bake at 350°F for 1 hour.

Nutritional Counter Per Serving:

Calories 355, Carbs 12.0g, Protein 25.0g, Fat 22.0g, Cholesterol 191mg, Sodium 476mg, Fiber 1.0g

Chicken Bacon Wraps

This bacon wrapped chicken goes well with hot rice.

Serves: 2

Preparation: 10 minutes

Total Time: 60 minutes

Ingredients:

2 chicken breast halves, boneless, skinless

4 slices bacon

1 (10.75 ounce) can condensed cream of mushroom soup

8 ounces sour cream

Directions:

1. Preheat the oven to 350°F. Coat rimmed sheet pan with cooking spray.

2. Wrap each chicken breast with 2 strips of bacon and place in greased pan.

3. Mix together the soup and sour cream in a bowl. Pour over the chicken,

4. Bake in the oven for 40-50 minutes. Remove from oven and let cool before serving.

Nutritional Counter Per Serving:

Calories 755, Carbs 15.5g, Protein 39.8g, Fat 59.5g, Cholesterol 157mg, Sodium 1587mg, Fiber 0.2g

Spicy Chicken Bites

Quick and easy tenders boosted with Indian flavors.

Serves: 2

Preparation: 5 minutes, plus marinating

Total Time: 30 minutes

Ingredients:

1/2 pound chicken tenderloins

1 tablespoon water

1/4 teaspoon curry powder

1/4 teaspoon crushed red pepper flakes

Dash ground turmeric

Dash ginger

Dash cinnamon

Dash paprika

1/4 teaspoon salt

Directions:

1. Combine the seasonings with water in a small bowl.

2. Brush mixture over the two sides of chicken. Place the chicken in the bowl and refrigerate for about 15 minutes

3. Coat a sheet pan with cooking spray and place chicken in the pan.

4. Broil 4 inches from the heat for 3 minutes. Flip over and broil on the other side for another 3 minutes.

Nutritional Counter Per Serving:

Calories 108, Carbs 1.0g, Protein 26.0g, Fat 1.0g, Cholesterol 67mg, Sodium 345mg, Fiber 0.2g

Barbeque Chicken Drumsticks

Serves: 3

Preparation: 10 minutes

Total Time: 70 minutes

Ingredients:

6 chicken drumsticks

1/3 cup ketchup

1/2 cup water

1/3 cup white vinegar

4 teaspoons butter

1/4 cup brown sugar

2 teaspoons dry mustard

2 teaspoons Worcestershire sauce

2 teaspoons salt

2 teaspoons chili powder

Directions:

1. Preheat the oven to 400°F.

2. Place drumsticks in a deep baking pan.

3. In a bowl, whisk together ketchup, water, vinegar, butter, brown sugar, mustard, Worcestershire sauce, salt and chili powder.

4. Pour the mixture over the chicken. Bake for 1 hour, until no longer pink at the bone. Turn drumsticks halfway through.

Nutritional Counter Per Serving:

Calories 443, Carbs 20.6g, Protein 39.2g, Fat 22.3g, Cholesterol 142mg, Sodium 2070mg, Fiber 0.8g

Crumbly Parmesan Chicken

Enjoy the mild flavor of Parmesan and herbs in this sumptuous chicken dish.

Serves: 2

Preparation: 10 minutes

Total Time: 55 minutes

Ingredients:

2 bone-in chicken breast halves

2 tablespoons grated Parmesan cheese

3 tablespoons dry bread crumbs

1 teaspoon dried oregano

1 teaspoon dried parsley flakes

1/4 teaspoon paprika

1/4 teaspoon salt

1/4 teaspoon pepper

1 tablespoon butter, melted

Directions:

1. Combine cheese, bread crumbs, oregano, parsley, paprika, salt and pepper in a shallow dish.

2. Brush the chicken with butter then coat with the crumb mixture.

3. Place in a rimmed sheet pan coated with cooking spray.

4. Bake, uncovered, for 45-50 minutes at 350°F.

Nutritional Counter Per Serving:

Calories 355, Carbs 6.0g, Protein 42.0g, Fat 17.0g, Cholesterol 129mg, Sodium 443mg, Fiber 1.0g

Herb Baked Chicken Breast

Serves: 2

Preparation: 10 minutes, plus marinating

Total Time: 1 hour 40 minutes

Ingredients:

2 bone-in, skin-on chicken breast halves

1/4 cup olive oil

1/2 teaspoon minced garlic

1/4 teaspoon dried basil

1/4 teaspoon dried rosemary

1/2 teaspoon sea salt

1/2 teaspoon cracked black pepper

Directions:

1. In a bowl, combine garlic, basil, rosemary, salt and pepper

2. Rub chicken with olive oil then rub with the spice mixture. Transfer to a sheet pan and refrigerate no less than 45 minutes.

3. Preheat your oven to 375°F. Bake chicken for 45-60 minutes or until no longer pink at the bone.

Nutritional Counter Per Serving:

Calories 615, Carbs 1.0g, Protein 54.5g, Fat 42.0g, Cholesterol 153mg, Sodium 567mg, Fiber 0.3g

Chicken Breast Cheese Rolls

An elegant dinner for the two of you on a special night.

Serves: 2

Preparation: 10 minutes

Total Time: 35 minutes

Ingredients:

2 chicken breast halves, boneless, skinless

2 tablespoons cream cheese, softened

1/4 cup shredded cheddar cheese

2 teaspoons chutney

1 tablespoon butter, melted

Directions:

1. Line a rimmed baking sheet with foil. Coat the foil with cooking spray.

2. Flatten chicken breasts to 1/4-inch thickness.

3. Combine cream cheese and cheddar cheese and spread over the chicken. Roll up chicken and secure with toothpicks.

4. Combine chutney and butter and spoon over the chicken.

5. Bake, uncovered, for 25-30 minutes at 350°F.

Nutritional Counter Per Serving:

Calories 251, Carbs 3.0g, Protein 21.0g, Fat 17.0g, Cholesterol 93mg, Sodium 228mg, Fiber 0.1g

Holiday Turkey For Two

Make this tasty recipe and enjoy the feelings and scents of the season.

Serves: 2

Preparation: 10 minutes

Total Time: 40 minutes

Ingredients:

2 (6-ounce) turkey breast tenderloins

1 tablespoon butter, melted

1/4 cup chicken broth

1/4 teaspoon paprika

1/4 teaspoon dried tarragon

1/4 teaspoon salt

1/2 cup sliced fresh mushrooms

Directions:

1. Coat a rimmed sheet pan with cooking spray and place turkey in it.

2. In a small bowl, mix together butter, broth, paprika, tarragon and salt. Spoon the mixture over turkey.

3. Arrange sliced mushrooms around turkey.

4. Bake, uncovered, for 30-35 minutes at 375°F. Baste occasionally with the pan drippings.

5. Remove and let stand for about 5 minutes before slicing. Serve along with pan drippings.

Nutritional Counter Per Serving:

Calories 260, Carbs 2.0g, Protein 39.8g, Fat 8.0g, Cholesterol 98mg, Sodium 428mg, Fiber 0.1g

Delightful Chicken Tenders

Serves: 2

Preparation: 5 minutes

Total Time: 45 minutes

Ingredients:

1 (9-ounce) package of chicken tenderloins

2 tablespoons of melted butter

1/2 cup of finely crushed dry stuffing mix

Directions:

1. Preheat your oven to 350°F.

2. Line a rimmed sheet pan with foil.

3. Rinse chicken, pat dry with paper towels and place on sheet pan.

4. Combine melted butter and stuffing mix. Place the mixture over the chicken.

4. Bake for 40 minutes in the oven.

Nutritional Counter Per Serving:

Calories 296, Carbs 10g, Protein 30.8g, Fat 13.6g, Cholesterol 103mg, Sodium 394mg, Fiber 0.5g

Crunchy Mustard Chicken

Golden baked chicken with a yummy, tangy taste.

Serves: 2

Preparation: 10 minutes

Total Time: 50 minutes

Ingredients:

2 bone-in chicken breast halves

1/4 cup plain yogurt

1/2 teaspoon Dijon mustard

1/2 teaspoon lemon juice

1/2 teaspoon salt-free herb seasoning blend

1/4 cup grated Parmesan cheese

1/2 cup cornflake crumbs

Directions:

1. In a shallow bowl, mix together yogurt, mustard, lemon juice and seasoning blend.

2. In another bowl, mix together the cheese and cornflake crumbs.

3. Roll chicken in the yogurt mixture and then in the crumb mixture.

4. Transfer to a greased sheet pan.

5. Bake, uncovered, for 35-45 minutes at 350°F.

Nutritional Counter Per Serving:

Calories 234, Carbs 20.0g, Protein 24.0g, Fat 6.3g, Cholesterol 57mg, Sodium 430mg, Fiber 0.2g

Tex-Mex Spicy Chicken

This is for you if you like your chicken hot.

Serves: 2

Preparation: 5 minutes

Total Time: 45 minutes

Ingredients:

4 chicken thighs

1 tablespoon brown sugar

1/2 cup Mexican-style hot sauce

1 tablespoon cayenne pepper

1 tablespoon paprika

Directions:

1. Preheat oven to 400°F. Coat a rimmed sheet pan with cooking spray.

2. In a bowl, mix together brown sugar, hot sauce, cayenne pepper and paprika.

3. Place chicken on the sheet pan, coat with a layer of the sauce then cover with foil.

4. Bake for 20 minutes in the oven. Remove the foil and bake for 20 minutes more.

Nutritional Counter Per Serving:

Calories 426, Carbs 11.2g, Protein 39.3g, Fat 24.8g, Cholesterol 142mg, Sodium 1610mg, Fiber 2.2g

SHEET PAN PORK RECIPES FOR TWO

Pork Tenderloin With Creamy Marinade

Serves: 2-3

Preparation: 10 minutes, plus marinating

Total Time: 55 minutes

Ingredients:

2 pounds pork tenderloin

1/4 cup soy sauce

1/4 cup olive oil

3 tablespoons of Dijon honey mustard

1 garlic clove, minced

Salt, to taste

Ground black pepper, to taste

Directions:

1. In a bowl, whisk together soy sauce, olive oil, mustard, garlic, salt and pepper. Pour into a large resealable bag.

2. Add pork to the resealable bag and refrigerator for a minimum of 1 hour.

3. Preheat your oven to 350°F.

4. Transfer the pork and the marinade into a rimmed baking sheet.

5. Bake for about 45 to 60 minutes, or until pork loin is no longer pink.

Nutritional Counter Per Serving:

Calories 485, Carbs 9.0g, Protein 55.3g, Fat 24.6g, Cholesterol 165mg, Sodium 1487mg, Fiber 0.7g

Baked Barbecue Ribs

Coat ribs with this zesty barbecue sauce to create a tender and flavorful outcome.

Serves: 2

Preparation: 10 minutes

Total Time: 1 hour 30 minutes

Ingredients:

2 pounds of pork baby back ribs, cut into bite size pieces

1/2 teaspoon garlic powder

2 tablespoons sugar

1/4 cup white vinegar

1/2 cup ketchup

1/2 teaspoon salt

1/4 teaspoon pepper

1/2 teaspoon paprika

3/4 teaspoon chili powder

1/2 teaspoon celery seed

1/2 teaspoon ground mustard

Directions:

1. Coat a rimmed sheet pan with cooking spray. Place ribs in the pan.

2. Rub pork ribs with garlic powder and bake, uncovered, for 45 minutes at 350°F.

3. In a small bowl, mix together the remaining ingredients.

4. Remove ribs from oven and drain. Pour half of the sauce over the meat. Return to oven and bake, uncovered, for about 40-50 minutes, basting at 10 minute intervals with the remaining sauce.

Nutritional Counter Per Serving:

Calories 890, Carbs 30.2g, Protein 51.7g, Fat 62.2g, Cholesterol 245mg, Sodium 1974mg, Fiber 1.0g

Cheesy Pork Chops Stuffed With Bacon And Chives

An easy way to get fancy dinner on the table in no time.

Serves: 2

Preparation: 15 minutes

Total Time: 35 minutes

Ingredients:

2 boneless pork loin chops, butterflied

2 slices cooked bacon, crumbled

4 ounces blue cheese, crumbled

2 tablespoons fresh chives, chopped

Black pepper, to taste

Garlic salt, to taste

Chopped fresh parsley for garnish

Directions:

1. Preheat your oven to 325°F. Coat baking sheet with cooking spray.

2. Mix together bacon, blue cheese and chives in a small bowl. Use your hands to form into 2 loose balls.

3. Place one ball each into the pocket of the butterflied pork chops. Fold and hold with toothpicks.

4. Rub pork chops all over with garlic salt and pepper. Don't use too much salt because blue cheese is salty.

5. Transfer to the greased baking sheet. Bake for 20-25 minutes.

Serve, garnished with parsley.

Nutritional Counter Per Serving:

Calories 393, Carbs 2.0g, Protein 36.0g, Fat 25.7g, Cholesterol 108mg, Sodium 1132mg, Fiber 0.4g

Pork With Zesty Horseradish Sauce

This zesty and sumptuous meal will always be appreciated.

Serves: 2

Preparation: 15 minutes

Total Time: 45 minutes

Ingredients:

1 pork tenderloin

1/2 teaspoon steak seasoning

1/2 teaspoon dried thyme

1/2 teaspoon dried rosemary, crushed

2 garlic cloves, peeled, quartered

1 teaspoon olive oil

1 teaspoon balsamic vinegar

For the sauce:

1 teaspoon prepared horseradish

2 tablespoons reduced-fat sour cream

2 tablespoons fat-free mayonnaise

Dash salt and pepper

1/8 teaspoon grated lemon peel

Directions:

1. Combine steak seasoning, thyme and rosemary in a small bowl. Rub pork with the mixture.

2. Use a sharp knife to cut 8 slits in the pork loin. Push a garlic quarter into each slit.

3. Line a sheet pan with foil, place meat on it and drizzle with olive oil and vinegar.

4. Bake for 30-40 minutes at 350°F. Remove and let stand for about 10 minutes before slicing.

5. Meanwhile, combine the ingredients for the sauce and refrigerate until serving.

Serve pork with sauce.

Nutritional Counter Per Serving:

Calories 258, Carbs 5.2g, Protein 35.0g, Fat 10.0g, Cholesterol 102mg, Sodium 451mg, Fiber 1.0g

Kaiser Roll Sandwich

Throw these sandwiches together quickly on weeknights when you don't have time to cook.

Serves: 2

Preparation: 5 minutes

Total Time: 20 minutes

Ingredients:

2 Kaiser rolls, split

2 tablespoons mayonnaise

1/4 cup of shredded reduced-fat cheddar cheese

4 slices of cooked bacon strips

6 slices deli ham

1/4 cup of shredded mozzarella cheese

Directions:

1. Spread rolls with mayonnaise.

2. Place roll bottoms on foil. Layer with cheese and bacon then follow with ham and mozzarella cheese. Cover with top.

3. Wrap sandwiches with foil and place on sheet pan.

4. Bake at 350°F for about 15-20 minutes.

Nutritional Counter Per Serving:

Calories 409, Carbs 33.0g, Protein 24.0g, Fat 20.0g, Cholesterol 53mg, Sodium 1184mg, Fiber 1.0g

Onion-Cola Pork Chops

Another great recipe for a hungry couple.

Serves: 2

Preparation: 5 minutes

Total Time: 65 minutes

Ingredients:

2 thick cut boneless pork chops

1 (1-ounce) envelope dry onion soup mix

1 (12-ounce) can cola-flavored carbonated beverage

Directions:

1. Preheat the oven to 350°F.

2. Place pork chops in a rimmed sheet pan.

3. Pour cola over the meat and sprinkle with the onion soup mix.

4. Bake uncovered in the oven for 30 minutes. Turn over and bake for 30 minutes more.

Nutritional Counter Per Serving:

Calories 234, Carbs 18.6g, Protein 22.2g, Fat 7.7g, Cholesterol 59mg, Sodium 865mg, Fiber 0.7g

Peach-Stuffed Pork Chops

A different taste from ordinary pork steaks.

Serves: 2

Preparation: 15 minutes

Total Time: 60 minutes

Ingredients:

2 bone-in center loin pork chops

1 (4-ounce) can diced peaches, undrained

1 cup instant chicken-flavored stuffing mix

1 tablespoon butter, melted

3 tablespoons hot water

1 tablespoon Dijon mustard

1/4 cup peach preserves

Directions:

1. Combine peaches, stuffing mix, butter and water in a small bowl.

2. Use a sharp knife to create a pocket in each pork chop. Do this by cutting almost to the bone.

3. Stuff each pocket with the peach mixture and hold with toothpicks.

4. Coat a rimmed sheet pan with cooking spray and place pork chops on it.

5. Mix together mustard and preserves and spread on pork chops.

6. Cover with foil and bake at 350°F for 30 minutes. Uncover and bake for 15-20 minutes more.

Nutritional Counter Per Serving:

Calories 507, Carbs 46.0g, Protein 40.7g, Fat 16.4g, Cholesterol 101mg, Sodium 541mg, Fiber 1.0g

Apricot-Stuffed Pork

This festive dish comes with a creamy texture and nutty flavor.

Serves: 2

Preparation: 20 minutes

Total Time: 50 minutes

Ingredients:

1 (3/4-pound) pork tenderloin

1/4 cup thinly sliced dried apricots

1/3 cup shredded Swiss cheese

1 small garlic clove, minced

1/4 teaspoon dried thyme

Dash cayenne pepper

1/4 teaspoon salt

Dash teaspoon pepper

1 tablespoon of butter, melted

Directions:

1. Cut a slit, lengthwise down the pork loin to within 1/2-inch of bottom.

2. Open tenderloin and let it lie flat. Cover with plastic wrap and use a mallet to flatten to about 1/2-inch thickness.

3. Sprinkle the meat with apricots, cheese, garlic, thyme, cayenne pepper, salt and pepper.

4. Roll up, starting with the long end. Tie with kitchen string at 2-inch intervals and use toothpicks to secure the ends.

5. Coat a sheet pan with cooking spray. Place tenderloin in the pan then brush with butter.

6. Bake at 375°F for 30-35 minutes. Remove and let cool for 5 minutes before slicing.

Nutritional Counter Per Serving:

Calories 374, Carbs 13.0g, Protein 39.4g, Fat 17.2g, Cholesterol 129mg, Sodium 462mg, Fiber 2.0g

Cheesy Hawaiian Pizza

Just half an hour, and this tasty dish is in your stomach.

Serves: 2

Preparation: 10 minutes

Total Time: 25 minutes

Ingredients:

2 (10-inches) flour tortillas

1-1/2 cups of shredded part-skim mozzarella cheese, divided

1/4 cup pizza sauce

3/4 cup diced fully cooked ham

1/2 cup pineapple tidbits, drained

Directions:

1. Coat a sheet pan with cooking spray.

2. Place a tortilla on the sheet pan and sprinkle with 1 cup of cheese. Top with the second tortilla then spread with pizza sauce.

3. Sprinkle with cooked ham, pineapple and the reserved cheese.

4. Bake for 15 minutes at 375°F. Tortillas should be crisp and cheese melted.

Nutritional Counter Per Serving:

Calories 636, Carbs 54.0g, Protein 41.0g, Fat 28.0g, Cholesterol 97mg, Sodium 855mg, Fiber 3.0g

Asian Spareribs

Get juicy, tender ribs on the table with this simple recipe.

Serves: 2

Preparation: 5 minutes

Total Time: 45 minutes

Ingredients:

1 pound pork spareribs

1 tablespoon ketchup

3 tablespoons hoisin sauce

1 tablespoon soy sauce

1 tablespoon honey

1 teaspoon rice vinegar

1 tablespoon sake

1 teaspoon lemon juice

1/4 teaspoon Chinese five-spice powder

1/2 teaspoon grated fresh garlic

1 teaspoon grated fresh ginger

Directions:

1. In a shallow glass dish, combine ketchup, hoisin sauce, soy sauce, honey, rice vinegar, sake, lemon juice, five-spice powder, garlic and fresh ginger.

2. Add the ribs to the marinade and turn to coat. Cover and place in the fridge for at least 2 hours.

3. Preheat the oven to 325°F. Cover the bottom of a rimmed sheet pan with water.

4. Place rack over sheet pan and arrange the ribs on the rack.

5. Place in the center of your oven and bake for 40 minutes. Turn and baste with marinade at 10 minutes, 20 minutes and 30 minutes. Discard remaining marinade.

Nutritional Counter Per Serving:

Calories 502, Carbs 23.0g, Protein 30.5g, Fat 31.0g, Cholesterol 121mg, Sodium 1016mg, Fiber 0.8g

Ham For Two

Lovely quick and easy ham slices.

Serves: 2

Preparation: 5 minutes

Total Time: 30 minutes

Ingredients:

2 small ham steaks

2 tablespoons crushed pineapple with juice

1 tablespoon brown sugar

Directions:

1. Line a sheet pan with foil.

2. Place ham in the pan and sprinkle with brown sugar.

3. Top with the crushed pineapple and bake for 20-25 minutes at 350°F.

Nutritional Counter Per Serving:

Calories 306, Carbs 23.3g, Protein 26.0g, Fat 12.0g, Cholesterol 75mg, Sodium 1816mg, Fiber 0.2g

Honey Mustard Pork

This delicious recipe goes well with baked sweet potato.

Serves: 2

Preparation: 15 minutes

Total Time: 1 hour 5 minutes

Ingredients:

2 boneless pork loin chops (1/2 inch thick)

1/4 teaspoon salt

1/8 teaspoon pepper

1/2 cup orange juice, divided

1 tablespoon all-purpose flour

1/4 teaspoon dried basil

1 tablespoon Dijon mustard

1/2 cup honey

1 small onion, sliced

2 medium carrots, diced

1/2 small sweet red pepper, cut into squares

1/2 small green pepper, cut into squares

Directions:

1. Season chops with salt and pepper then place in a deep pan.

2. In a small bowl, whisk 2 tablespoons of orange juice with the flour until smooth. Whisk in the remaining orange juice, basil, mustard and honey.

3. Pour mixture over pork chops. Arrange onion and carrots around the meat.

4. Cover and bake for 30 minutes at 350°F.

5. Add peppers, cover then bake for another 20 minutes.

Nutritional Counter Per Serving:

Calories 586, Carbs 92.0g, Protein 35.0g, Fat 11.3g, Cholesterol 83mg, Sodium 555mg, Fiber 4.0g

Juicy Ham And Sweet Potatoes

A sumptuous dish you can eat anytime of the year.

Serves: 2

Preparation: 5 minutes

Total Time: 45 minutes

Ingredients:

2 ham steaks

1/4 cup of packed brown sugar

1 (15-ounce) can of sweet potatoes, drained

1 (8-ounce) can of crushed pineapple, drained

1 cup of miniature marshmallows

Directions:

1. Preheat your oven to 350°F.

2. Place each ham slice on a large piece of foil.

3. Sprinkle each with a little brown sugar, spread some crushed pineapple over then top with the sweet potatoes. Layer the remaining brown sugar and then pineapple.

4. Fold foil packets tightly and place on sheet pan.

5. Bake in the oven for 30 minutes.

6. Remove packets from the oven and open carefully. Sprinkle with miniature marshmallows and return to the

oven without closing the foil packets. Bake for 10 minutes more.

Serve with a side of vegetables.

Nutritional Counter Per Serving:

Calories 511, Carbs 110.4g, Protein 13.2g, Fat 2.6g, Cholesterol 27mg, Sodium 860mg, Fiber 4.7g

SHEET PAN BEEF AND OTHER MEAT RECIPES FOR TWO

Braised Lamb Shanks

A treat for lovers of lamb shanks.

Serves: 2

Preparation: 10 minutes

Total Time: 2 hour 10 minutes

Ingredients:

2 lamb shanks

1/4 cup soy sauce

1 cup beef broth

2 teaspoons prepared mustard

1 garlic clove, minced

2 tablespoons brown sugar

Directions:

1. Place lamb in a grease rimmed sheet pan.

2. In a bowl, mix together soy sauce, beef broth, mustard, garlic and brown sugar. Pour over lamb.

3. Cover with foil and bake at 325°F for 1-1/2 to 2 hours.

Nutritional Counter Per Serving:

Calories 450, Carbs 15.0g, Protein 48.0g, Fat 21.0g, Cholesterol 160mg, Sodium 2417mg, Fiber 0.1g

Chinese Beef Strips

Enjoy the delicious Asian flavor of sirloin strips marinated in sake and soy sauce. You can serve it with hot cooked rice if desired.

Serves: 2

Preparation: 5 minutes, plus marinating

Total Time: 15 minutes

Ingredients:

1/2 pound beef top sirloin steak

1/4 cup reduced-sodium soy sauce

2 tablespoons unsweetened apple juice

2 green onions, sliced thinly

4 garlic cloves, minced

3 tablespoons sugar

1 teaspoon sesame oil

1 tablespoon sesame seeds

1/4 teaspoon pepper

Directions:

1. Cut steak into 1/4-inch strips then flatten to 1/8-inch thickness.

2. In a large Ziploc bag, combine soy sauce, apple juice, onions, garlic, sugar, sesame oil, sesame seeds and pepper. Add the beef, seal the bag and shake gently to coat. Marinate in refrigerator for at least 1 hour.

3. Preheat broiler. Drain beef and discard the marinade. Place beef on a sheet pan.

4. Broil 3-4 inches from heat for about 2-3 minutes on each side.

Nutritional Counter Per Serving:

Calories 195, Carbs 8.0g, Protein 23.3g, Fat 7.0g, Cholesterol 63mg, Sodium 435mg, Fiber 0.2g

Yummy Steak

Serves: 2

Preparation: 5 minutes

Total Time: 21 minutes

Ingredients:

1 (1/2-pound) frozen rib-eye steak

1 tablespoon butter, divided

1 tablespoon of Worcestershire sauce

1 teaspoon of meat tenderizer

Salt and black pepper to taste

1 garlic clove, minced

Directions:

1. Preheat oven broiler.

2. Place frozen steak on sheet pan. Spread half of the butter on the meat. Pour Worcestershire sauce over, then sprinkle generously with tenderizer, salt, pepper and garlic.

3. Broil about 6-8 minutes. Remove from the oven, flip to other side, spread with butter and sprinkle with seasonings as before.

4. Return to broiler and cook again for about 6-8 minutes.

Nutritional Counter Per Serving:

Calories 214, Carbs 2.2g, Protein 12.7g, Fat 16.4g,
Cholesterol 56mg, Sodium 405mg, Fiber 0g

Roast Beef With Potatoes And Bok Choy

Serves: 2

Preparation: 20 minutes

Total Time: 1 hour 30 minutes

Ingredients:

1 pound top loin roast

Kosher salt, to taste

Black pepper, to taste

1 head baby bok choy, quartered

1 russet potatoes, cut into 8 1-inch wedges

1 tablespoons canola oil

1 scallion, chopped roughly

1/4 cup mayonnaise

Directions:

1. Preheat your oven to 425°F.

2. Place meat in a sheet pan and season with salt and pepper (about 1/2 teaspoon each). Roast for about 18-22 minutes

3. In a large bowl, toss bok choy, potatoes, canola oil and 1/8 teaspoon each of salt and pepper. Add mixture to sheet pan.

4. Continue roasting for 20-25 minutes more

5. Slice meat. Serve with potatoes and bok choy then top with scallions and mayo.

Nutritional Counter Per Serving:

Calories 630, Carbs 34.0g, Protein 48.7g, Fat 32.6g, Cholesterol 105mg, Sodium 840mg, Fiber 3.0g

Meat Loaf For One

Simply combine the vegetables with ground beef and have a nourishing meal.

Serves: 1

Preparation: 10 minutes

Total Time: 45 minutes

Ingredients:

1/4 pound ground beef

1/2 slice bread, crumbled

2 tablespoons finely shredded carrot

1 tablespoon chopped green pepper

1 tablespoon each chopped onion

1 tablespoon chopped celery

1/4 teaspoon salt

Dash pepper

2 tablespoons ketchup, divided

Directions:

1. In a bowl, mix together carrot, green pepper, onion, celery, salt, pepper and 1 tablespoon ketchup.

2. Add beef, mix well with your hands and then shape into a 3 x 2-inch loaf.

3. Place on a an ungreased sheet pan and top with remaining ketchup.

4. Bake, uncovered, for 35-40 minutes at 350°F.

Nutritional Counter Per Serving:

Calories 299, Carbs 17.0g, Protein 24.0g, Fat 14.3g, Cholesterol 76mg, Sodium 1182mg, Fiber 1.0g

Flat Iron Steak With Potatoes And Lemon

Serves: 2

Preparation: 10 minutes

Total Time: 65 minutes

Ingredients:

12 ounces flat iron steak

2 tablespoons olive oil

12 ounces new potatoes, halved

4 sprigs thyme

1/2 teaspoon chili powder

Kosher salt, to taste

Pepper, to taste

1/2 lemon, quartered

Directions:

1. Preheat your oven to 425°F.

2. In a sheet pan, toss olive oil, potatoes, thyme, chili powder, salt and pepper.

3. Roast in oven for about, 40-45 minutes, stirring once halfway through. Transfer to plates.

4. Heat the broiler. Wipe sheet pan with paper towels. Season steak with some salt and pepper. Place on sheet pan and broil for about 4 minutes per side. Remove from oven and let rest for a few minutes before slicing.

7. Serve steak with potatoes and lemon.

Nutritional Counter Per Serving:

Calories , Carbs 31.0g, Protein 48.7g, Fat 16.7g,
Cholesterol 99mg, Sodium 1084mg, Fiber 4.0g

Creamy Meatballs

Serves: 2

Preparation: 10 minutes

Total Time: 50 minutes

Ingredients:

1/2 pound lean ground beef

1/2 cup grated peeled potato

1/4 cup dry bread crumbs

2 tablespoons beaten egg

2 tablespoons finely chopped onion

1/4 teaspoon pepper, divided

1/8 teaspoon garlic powder

2/3 cup condensed cream of mushroom soup

3/4 cup water

1/2 cup sour cream

4-1/2 teaspoons onion soup mix

1/3 cup canned mushroom stems and pieces, drained

Directions:

1. In a small bowl, mix together potato, bread crumbs, egg, onion, 1/8 teaspoon pepper and garlic. Crumble the beef into the mixture and mix well.

2. Shape into 1-1/2-inch meatballs then place in a greased rimmed sheet pan.

3. In a small bowl, mix together cream of mushroom soup, water, sour cream, onion soup, mushroom and remaining pepper. Pour mixture over meatballs.

4. Bake, uncovered, for 30-40 minutes at 350°F.

Nutritional Counter Per Serving:

Calories 297, Carbs 22.0g, Protein 22.4g, Fat 12.8g, Cholesterol 135mg, Sodium 1050mg, Fiber 1.0g

Lamb Shanks With Mixed Herbs

Serves: 2

Preparation: 5 minutes

Total Time: 30 minutes

Ingredients:

2 lamb shanks

1 tablespoon olive oil

1 tablespoon minced fresh parsley

2 garlic cloves, minced

1/2 teaspoon dried thyme

1/2 teaspoon dried rosemary, crushed

Directions:

1. Preheat the oven to 400°F.

2. In a bowl, mix together olive oil, parsley, garlic, thyme and rosemary. Rub the mixture over lamb.

3. Place the meat on a rack in a greased sheet pan.

4. Bake, uncovered, for 20-30 minutes

Nutritional Counter Per Serving:

Calories 241, Carbs 1.0g, Protein 21.0g, Fat 17.0g, Cholesterol 67mg, Sodium 63mg, Fiber 0.2g

Weeknight Chopped Steak

You will always want more of this hamburger steak.

Serves: 2

Preparation: 5 minutes

Total Time: 20 minutes

Ingredients:

3/4 pound ground beef

3/4 cup soft bread crumbs

1 egg, beaten

1/4 cup finely chopped onion

1 1/2 teaspoons Worcestershire sauce

1/4 teaspoon salt

1/8 teaspoon pepper

Directions:

1. In a bowl, mix together bread crumbs, egg, onion, Worcestershire sauce, salt and pepper.

2. Shape the mixture into two patties, about 1/2 inch thick.

3. Place in a sheet pan and broil for about 5-7 minutes on each side.

Nutritional Counter Per Serving:

Calories 425, Carbs 11.3g, Protein 37.8g, Fat 24.3g, Cholesterol 219mg, Sodium 541mg, Fiber 1.0g

SHEET PAN VEGETABLES RECIPES FOR TWO

Roasted Tomato Sandwich

This sandwich goes well with a bowl of soup.

Serves: 2

Preparation: 10 minutes

Total Time: 15 minutes

Ingredients:

4 slices of bread, toasted lightly

4 ripe tomatoes, sliced

2 tablespoons balsamic vinegar

2 tablespoons olive oil

3 tablespoons mayonnaise

1/4 teaspoon black pepper

1/4 teaspoon dried oregano

1/2 teaspoon dried parsley

3 tablespoons of grated Parmesan cheese, divided

Directions:

1. Preheat your oven to broil.

2. In a small bowl, whisk together vinegar and olive oil. Add the tomatoes and let marinate for several minutes.

3. Meanwhile, in another bowl, mix together mayonnaise, black pepper, oregano, parsley and 1 1/2 tablespoons of cheese.

4. Arrange slices of toasted bread on a baking sheet. Spread each slice with the mayonnaise mixture. Place the tomatoes on 2 slices and sprinkle with reserved cheese.

5. Broil for about 5 minutes or until cheese becomes light brown.

Serve sandwich closed.

Nutritional Counter Per Serving:

Calories 509, Carbs 43.2g, Protein 9.6g, Fat 34.7g, Cholesterol 14mg, Sodium 604mg, Fiber 4.8g

Seasoned Oven Fries

Oven fried potatoes with a difference.

Serves: 2

Preparation: 5 minutes

Total Time: 30 minutes

Ingredients:

2 medium baking potatoes

2 teaspoons canola oil

2 teaspoons butter, melted

1/4 teaspoon seasoned salt

Directions:

1. Cut potatoes in half lengthwise then cut each half into four wedges.

2. Combine the other ingredients in a large resealable bag. Add potatoes and shake to coat.

3. Coat a sheet pan with cooking spray then arrange potatoes in a single layer.

4. Bake for 20-25 minutes at 450°F, turning once.

Nutritional Counter Per Serving:

Calories 263, Carbs 44.2g, Protein 4.0g, Fat 9.1g, Cholesterol 10.0mg, Sodium 242mg, Fiber 4.0g

Eggplant Sandwich

This roasted eggplant in French roll can easily become a favorite.

Serves: 2

Preparation: 20 minutes

Total Time: 30 minutes

Ingredients:

1 small eggplant, halved, sliced

1 tablespoon of olive oil

2 (6-inch) French sandwich rolls

2 garlic cloves, minced

1/4 cup mayonnaise

1/2 cup crumbled feta cheese

1 small tomato, sliced

1/4 cup of chopped fresh basil leaves

Directions:

1. Preheat broiler. Brush the slices of eggplant with olive oil and place on sheet pan.

2. Set sheet pan 6 inches from broiler. Broil for 10 minutes.

3. Meanwhile, divide French rolls lengthwise, then toast.

4. Stir together garlic and mayo in a small bowl. Spread mixture on toasted French rolls.

5. Fill rolls with eggplant slices, feta cheese, tomato and basil. Serve.

Nutritional Counter Per Serving:

Calories 803, Carbs 91.3g, Protein 23.7g, Fat 39.6g, Cholesterol 44mg, Sodium 1460mg, Fiber 8g

Butternut Squash Stuffed With Rice

Enjoy the exotic flavor of butternut, cranberries, mango chutney and rice. Use it as side dish or light evening meal.

Serves: 2

Preparation: 40 minutes

Total Time: 55 minutes

Ingredients:

1 small butternut squash

3/4 cup cooked long grain rice

3 tablespoons mango chutney

3 tablespoons dried cranberries

3/4 teaspoon curry powder

1/3 cup ricotta cheese

1 green onion, chopped

2 teaspoons butter

1/4 teaspoon salt

1/4 teaspoon pepper

Directions:

1. Cut the butternut squash into half lengthwise. Remove and discard seeds.

2. Cut off a thin slice from the bottom of the halves so they can sit flat.

3. Place each half cut side down in a rimmed sheet pan. Add about 1/2 inch of water. Bake, uncovered, for 30 minutes at 350°F.

4. Drain water from the pan and let cool. Turn the squash cut side up then scoop out the pulp, leaving a shell of about 1/4 inch.

5. Combine the other ingredients (except butter) in a large bowl. Spoon the mixture into the squash shells then top with butter.

6. Return to the oven and bake for about 15-20 minutes.

Nutritional Counter Per Serving:

Calories 386, Carbs 82.3g, Protein 9.3g, Fat 4.0g, Cholesterol 17mg, Sodium 906mg, Fiber 11.3g

Portobello Mushrooms In Asian Marinade

Enjoy these Asian-flavored Portobello mushrooms.

Serves: 2

Preparation: 10 minutes

Total Time: 43 minutes

Ingredients:

2 large Portobello mushroom caps

1 tablespoon olive oil

1/2 cup cooking wine

2 tablespoons balsamic vinegar

2 tablespoons dark soy sauce

2 garlic cloves, minced

Directions:

1. Preheat your oven to 400°F.

2. In a sheet pan, mix together olive oil, wine, balsamic vinegar, soy sauce and garlic.

3. Place the mushroom caps upside down in the mixture and let marinate for about 15 minutes.

4. Cover and bake for 25 minutes then turn mushrooms and bake for 8 minutes more.

Serve on hamburger buns or as steaks.

Nutritional Counter Per Serving:

Calories 112, Carbs 4.5g, Protein 1.3g, Fat 6.7g, Cholesterol 0mg, Sodium 1286mg, Fiber 0.2g

Tortilla Chips With Herbs

Healthy, inexpensive and delicious.

Serves: 3

Preparation: 10 minutes

Total Time: 17 minutes

Ingredients:

2 (6-inch) flour tortillas

2 teaspoons olive oil

1/4 teaspoon garlic powder

1/2 teaspoon dried oregano

1/2 teaspoon dried rosemary, crushed

1/2 teaspoon dried parsley flakes

2 teaspoons grated Parmesan cheese

1/8 teaspoon kosher salt

1/8 teaspoon pepper

Directions:

1. In a small bowl, combine garlic powder, oregano, rosemary, parsley, Parmesan cheese, salt and pepper.

2. Cut each tortilla into six wedges and brush the with oil. Coat a sheet pan with cooking spray and arrange tortillas in a single layer.

3. Sprinkle with season mixture then bake for 5-7 minutes at 425°F. Remove from oven and let cool for 5 minutes.

Nutritional Counter Per Serving:

Calories 93, Carbs 9.0g, Protein 3.2g, Fat 5.3g, Cholesterol 1mg, Sodium 245mg, Fiber 0.2g

Baked Zucchini

Serve this with your favorite meat for a complete meal.

Serves: 2

Preparation: 10 minutes

Total Time: 45 minutes

Ingredients:

2 medium zucchini, cut into 1/4-inch slices

1 tablespoon of minced fresh oregano

2 tablespoons of butter, melted

1/4 cup of grated Parmesan cheese

Salt to taste

Pepper to taste

Directions:

1. In a large bowl, combine zucchini with oregano and butter. Toss to coat.

2. Coat a sheet pan with cooking spray. Arrange zucchini in a single layer and sprinkle with Parmesan cheese.

3. Bake, uncovered, for 35-40 minutes at 350°F.

Season with salt and pepper and serve with chosen entree.

Nutritional Counter Per Serving:

Calories 117, Carbs 4.0g, Protein 4.0g, Fat 10.3g, Cholesterol 26mg, Sodium 204mg, Fiber 2.0g

Baked Sugar Snap Peas

This quick and easy sugar snap peas goes well with a variety of main dishes.

Serves: 2

Preparation: 5 minutes

Total Time: 15 minutes

Ingredients:

1 (8-ounce) package fresh sugar snap peas

1/2 teaspoon Italian seasoning

1 tablespoon chopped shallot

2 teaspoons olive oil

1/8 teaspoon salt

Directions:

1. Place peas in a sheet pan.

2. Combine the other ingredients in a bowl, drizzle over peas then toss to coat.

3. Bake, uncovered, for 8-10 minutes at 400°F. Stir once.

Nutritional Counter Per Serving:

Calories 92, Carbs 9.3g, Protein 4.2g, Fat 5.0g, Cholesterol 0mg, Sodium 154mg, Fiber 2.8g

Cheesy Baked Potatoes

Make a sure winner tonight with these yummy, delicious potatoes.

Serves: 2

Preparation: 20 minutes

Total Time: 1 hour 20 minutes

Ingredients:

2 medium baking potatoes

1 tablespoon 2% milk

2 tablespoons butter, softened

1/4 teaspoon salt

2 tablespoons sour cream

1 (3-ounce) package cream cheese, cubed

Paprika, to taste

Directions:

1. Pierce the potatoes then transfer to a sheet pan. Bake for 1 hour at 375°. Remove from oven and let cool.

2. Cut off a thin slice at the top of each potato. Use a spoon to scoop out the pulp, leaving the thin shell.

3. In a bowl, combine the pulp with milk, butter and salt. Mash well then stir in sour cream and cream cheese. Spoon the mixture back into the shells then sprinkle with paprika.

4. Return potatoes to sheet pan. Bake, uncovered, for 20-25 minutes at 350°F.

Nutritional Counter Per Serving:

Calories 450, Carbs 40g, Protein 8.0g, Fat 29.0g, Cholesterol 89mg, Sodium 560mg, Fiber 3.0g

Roasted Eggplant Salad

Serves: 2

Preparation: 15 minutes

Total Time: 55 minutes

Ingredients:

1 large eggplant

Kosher salt

1 tablespoons cider vinegar

3 tablespoons olive oil

2 teaspoon honey

Dash cumin

1/2 teaspoon smoked paprika

2 large garlic cloves, chopped roughly

2 teaspoon soy sauce

Juice of 1/2 lemon, about 1 tablespoon

1/4 cup smoked almonds, chopped roughly

1/2 cup flat parsley leaves,

1/4 cup scallions, chopped finely

1 ounce goat cheese, crumbled, divided

Directions:

1. Preheat oven to 400°F.

2. Cut eggplant into 1-inch cubes, place in a large bowl and sprinkle lightly with salt.

3. In a bowl, whisk together vinegar, olive oil, honey, cumin, paprika and garlic.

4. Pat eggplant cubes with paper towels to remove water and combine eggplant with the marinade.

5. Line a sheet pan with parchment then spread the eggplant on it. Place on the center rack in the preheated oven and bake for 35-40 minutes, stirring every 15 minutes. Remove from the oven and let cool for a few minutes.

6. Whisk together the soy sauce and lemon juice. Toss mixture with baked eggplant then stir in smoked almonds, parsley and 3/4 of the cheese.

7. Serve, sprinkled with scallions and remaining goat cheese.

Nutritional Counter Per Serving:

Calories 355, Carbs 23.4g, Protein 8.6g, Fat 28.0g, Cholesterol 7mg, Sodium 295mg, Fiber 10.3g

Roasted Peppers And Fresh Basil

Treat yourself to the sweet, smoky flavor of roasting peppers.

Serves: 2

Preparation: 10 minutes, plus standing

Total Time: 20 minutes

Ingredients:

1 each medium green, sweet yellow and red pepper

1 garlic clove, minced

9 fresh basil leaves, sliced thinly

1-1/2 teaspoons of balsamic vinegar

1/8 teaspoon salt

Directions:

1. Place peppers on sheet pan and broil, 4 inches from heat for 6-8 minutes. Rotate every 1-2 minutes so that all sides are evenly blackened and blistered. Transfer peppers to a bowl, cover and set aside for 15 minutes.

2. After 15 minutes, peel off and discard the skin of the peppers then remove seeds and stems.

3. Slice peppers into 1/4-inch strips and transfer to a bowl.

4. Add garlic, basil, vinegar and salt then toss to coat.

5. Cover and set aside for 30 minutes before serving.

Nutritional Counter Per Serving:

Calories 53, Carbs 13.0g, Protein 2.0g, Fat 0g, Cholesterol 0mg, Sodium 151mg, Fiber 3.0g

Roasted Carrots, Chickpeas And Parsnips

Serves: 2

Preparation: 10 minutes

Total Time: 40 minutes

Ingredients:

4 ounces parsnips

8 ounces carrots

2 tablespoons olive oil, divided

1/8 teaspoon coarse kosher salt

1 teaspoons chili powder

1/4 cup of cooked chickpeas

2 teaspoons of pomegranate molasses

1 ounce feta cheese, crumbled

2 teaspoons chopped flat-leaf parsley

Directions:

1. Preheat the oven to 400°F

2. Scrub carrots and parsnips. Halve carrots lengthwise then cut parsnips to match carrot size.

3. Toss parsnips and carrots with 1 tablespoon olive oil, salt and chili powder.

4. Spread, single layer on a rimmed sheet pan. Place in the oven to roast.

5. Add the remaining olive oil to chickpeas and toss. After 15 minutes, turn the parsnips and carrots then add chickpeas. Roast for 10 minutes more.

6. Toss with pomegranate molasses and roast for 5 minutes more.

7. Remove from oven then toss with parsley and feta cheese.

Nutritional Counter Per Serving:

Calories 265, Carbs 31.0g, Protein 5.5g, Fat 14.2g, Cholesterol 13mg, Sodium 439mg, Fiber 7.5g

SHEET PAN SEAFOOD RECIPES FOR TWO

One Pan Broiled Scallops

Get the taste of 5-star scallops right in your own home.

Serves: 2-3

Preparation: 5 minutes

Total Time: 13 minutes

Ingredients:

1 1/2 pounds of bay scallops

1 tablespoon of garlic salt

2 tablespoons of lemon juice

2 tablespoons margarine, melted

Directions:

1. Preheat your oven to broil.

2. Rinse scallops and place in a sheet pan.

3. Season scallops with garlic salt then drizzle with lemon juice and margarine.

4. Broil for about 6-8 minutes or until scallops begin to turn light brown.

Serve with extra melted margarine for dipping.

Nutritional Counter Per Serving:

Calories 273, Carbs 6.8 g, Protein 38.3 g, Fat 9.4 g, Cholesterol 95 mg, Sodium 2232 mg, Fiber 0.1 g

Foil Wrapped Rainbow Trout
Finger-licking and simply delicious!

Serves: 2

Preparation: 10 minutes

Total Time: 30 minutes

Ingredients:

2 rainbow trout fillets

1 tablespoon of olive oil

1 teaspoon ground black pepper

2 teaspoons of garlic salt

1 fresh jalapeno pepper, sliced

1 lemon, sliced

Directions:

1. Preheat the oven to 400°F.

2. Rinse the fish and pat dry with paper towels.

3. Rub fish with oil and sprinkle with garlic salt and black pepper.

4. Place fillets on separate sheet of foil and top with slices of jalapeno.

5. Squeeze juice from the lemon slices on the fillets and then arrange lemon slices on the fish.

6. Fold the foil into packets and place on sheet pan.

7. Bake for 15-20 minutes or until fish flakes easily with a fork.

Nutritional Counter Per Serving:

Calories 213, Carbs 7.5g, Protein 24.3g, Fat 10.9g, Cholesterol 67mg, Sodium 1850mg, Fiber 2.8g

Spicy Baked Catfish

Moist and flaky fish with a crisp and spicy coating.

Serves: 2

Preparation: 5 minutes

Total Time: 30 minutes

Ingredients:

2 (6-ounce) catfish fillets

2 tablespoons cornmeal

1/2 teaspoon dried thyme

1/4 teaspoon garlic powder

1/2 teaspoon dried basil

1/4 teaspoon lemon-pepper seasoning

2 teaspoons blackening seasoning

1/4 teaspoon paprika

Directions:

1. Preheat the oven to 400°F.

2. In a large resealable bag, combine cornmeal, thyme, garlic powder, dried basil, lemon-pepper and blackening seasoning.

3. Add the catfish fillets and shake to coat well.

4. Coat a sheet pan with cooking spray. Place catfish fillets on the pan and sprinkle with paprika.

5. Bake for about 20-25 minutes or until fish flakes easily with a fork.

Nutritional Counter Per Serving:

Calories 265, Carbs 8.0g, Protein 27.0g, Fat 12.9g, Cholesterol 82mg, Sodium 812mg, Fiber 1.0g

Rosemary Lemon Salmon

A simple and impressive meal for a romantic night.

Serves: 2

Preparation: 10 minutes

Total Time: 30 minutes

Ingredients:

2 salmon fillets, skin and bones removed

4 sprigs fresh rosemary

1 lemon, sliced thinly

Salt to taste

1 tablespoon olive oil

Directions:

1. Preheat the oven to 400°F.

2. In a sheet pan, arrange half the lemon slices in single layer. Next, layer 2 rosemary sprigs then top with the salmon fillets.

3. Sprinkle salt on salmon fillets, layer the remaining sprigs of rosemary then top with remaining slices of lemon. Drizzle all with olive oil.

4. Place in oven and bake for 20 minutes.

Nutritional Counter Per Serving:

Calories 257, Carbs 6.2g, Protein 20.5g, Fat 18.0g, Cholesterol 55mg, Sodium 1016mg, Fiber 2.6g

Lobster Tails Sheet Pan Dinner

This simple preparation easily brings out the natural flavor of lobster.

Serves: 2

Preparation: 15 minutes

Total Time: 20 minutes

Ingredients:

1/2 cup butter, melted

2 whole lobster tails

1/2 teaspoon ground paprika

Salt and ground white pepper, to taste

1 lemon, cut into wedges, for garnish

Directions:

1. Preheat oven broiler.

2. In a bowl, mix together butter, paprika, salt and white pepper.

3. Place the lobster tails on a sheet pan.

4. Using a sharp knife, cut the top part of the lobster shells lengthwise. Slightly pull apart and season with the butter and pepper mixture.

5. Broil for 5-10 minutes, or until lobster is browned and opaque.

Serve, garnished with lemon wedges.

Nutritional Counter Per Serving:

Calories 590, Carbs 7.4g, Protein 37.0g, Fat 48.0g, Cholesterol 303mg, Sodium 892mg, Fiber 2.8g

Tilapia With Mustard Crust

This simple recipe will wow you every time.

Serves: 2

Preparation: 5 minutes

Total Time: 20 minutes

Ingredients:

2 (6-ounce) fresh tilapia fillets

1 teaspoon Worcestershire sauce

1 teaspoon spicy brown mustard

1/2 teaspoon lemon juice

1/4 teaspoon dried oregano

1/4 teaspoon garlic powder

1/2 teaspoon of grated Parmesan cheese

1 teaspoon of fine Italian bread crumbs

Directions:

1. Preheat the oven to 375°F. Spray baking sheet with cooking spray.

2. Place fish on the baking sheet and bake for 10 minutes.

3. In the meantime, combine Worcestershire sauce, mustard, lemon juice, oregano, garlic powder and Parmesan cheese. Stir together.

4. When fish is 10 minutes in the oven, spread with the mustard and spice paste and sprinkle with bread crumbs.

5. Bake for 5 more minutes or until topping is golden and bubbly.

Nutritional Counter Per Serving:

Calories 182, Carbs 2.0g, Protein 35.1g, Fat 2.6g, Cholesterol 62mg, Sodium 149mg, Fiber 0.2g

Salmon With Tomato-Tarragon Sauce

Salmon turns out nicely with this sauce.

Serves: 2

Preparation: 10 minutes

Total Time: 35 minutes

Ingredients:

2 (6-ounce) salmon fillets

1-1/2 teaspoons milk

1/3 cup mayonnaise

1/4 teaspoon tarragon

1/2 teaspoon lemon-pepper seasoning

1 plum tomato, diced

Directions:

1. Spray a sheet pan with cooking spray.

2. Place salmon in the pan and bake at 350°F for 20-25 minutes.

3. In a small bowl, stir together milk, mayonnaise, tarragon, lemon-pepper seasoning and tomato.

4. Spoon sauce over salmon then bake for 5 minutes more.

Nutritional Counter Per Serving:

Calories 432, Carbs 2.0g, Protein 17.0g, Fat 39.0g, Cholesterol 64mg, Sodium 370mg, Fiber 0.2g

Honey Coconut Tilapia

Serves: 2

Preparation: 10 minutes

Total Time: 55 minutes

Ingredients:

2 (3-ounce) fillets tilapia

3 tablespoons coconut aminos

3 tablespoons honey

3 tablespoons balsamic vinegar

1 tablespoon minced garlic

Cooking spray

1 teaspoon of freshly cracked black pepper

Directions:

1. In a bowl, mix together coconut aminos, honey, balsamic vinegar and garlic.

2. Place fish in the mixture and place in the fridge to marinate for at least 30 minutes.

3. Preheat your oven to 350°F. Coat a sheet pan with cooking spray.

4. Remove fillets from the marinade, then discard the marinade.

5. Transfer fish to the greased sheet pan and sprinkle with black pepper.

6. Bake for about 15-20 minutes or until fish flakes easily with a fork.

Nutritional Counter Per Serving:

Calories 218, Carbs 33.2g, Protein 19.3g, Fat 1.4g, Cholesterol 31mg, Sodium 1398mg, Fiber 0.6g

Cod With Mixed Vegetables

Warm your body with this nourishing meal on chilly evenings.

Serves: 2

Preparation: 15 minutes

Total Time: 40 minutes

Ingredients:

2 (6-ounce) cod fillets

2 cups broccoli coleslaw mix

4 teaspoons chopped green onion

1/2 cup chopped fresh tomato

2 garlic cloves, minced

Pepper to taste

3 tablespoons seasoned bread crumbs

1/4 cup crushed potato sticks

4 teaspoons butter, melted

2 tablespoons grated Parmesan cheese

Directions:

1. Coat a deep pan with cooking spray.

2. In a large bowl, mix together coleslaw mix, green onion, tomato and garlic. Spread into the prepared pan.

3. Add the cod fillets and sprinkle with pepper.

4. Mix together bread crumbs, potato sticks, butter and cheese. Sprinkle over cod fillets.

5. Bake, uncovered, for 25-30 minutes at 450°F.

Nutritional Counter Per Serving:

Calories 316, Carbs 18.0g, Protein 34.0g, Fat 12.0g, Cholesterol 89mg, Sodium 444mg, Fiber 3g

Basil Tomato Salmon

Serve this with a side of greens and a bottle of wine for the perfect weeknight dinner.

Serves: 2

Preparation: 10 minutes

Total Time: 30 minutes

Ingredients:

2 (6-ounce) boneless salmon fillets

1 tomato, sliced thinly

1 tablespoon dried basil

1 tablespoon of olive oil

2 tablespoons of grated Parmesan cheese

Directions:

1. Preheat oven to 375°F.

2. Line a sheet pan with foil then coat with cooking spray.

3. Place salmon fillets on the foil, top with slices of tomato, sprinkle with basil, drizzle with the olive oil. Finally top with Parmesan cheese.

4. Bake in the oven for about 20 minutes, or until fish is opaque and cheese is golden brown on top.

Nutritional Counter Per Serving:

Calories 405, Carbs 4.0g, Protein 36.2g, Fat 26.6g, Cholesterol 104mg, Sodium 180mg, Fiber 1.5g

Garlicky Spicy Salmon

Get more out of salmon with this delicious and spicy paste.

Serves: 2

Preparation: 10 minutes

Total Time: 25 minutes

Ingredients:

2 (6-ounce) fillets salmon

1 dried red chili pepper

2 garlic cloves, crushed

1 tablespoon olive oil

2 tablespoons fresh lime juice

1 teaspoon whole grain mustard

Sea salt to taste

Freshly ground black pepper

Directions:

1. Preheat oven to 400°F. Line a rimmed sheet pan with aluminum foil. Spray foil lightly with cooking spray.

2. Grind together chili pepper and garlic using a mortar and pestle. Combine with olive oil, lime juice, mustard, salt and pepper, to make a paste.

3. Place salmon in the prepared sheet pan then coat with the paste.

4. Bake for 12-15 minutes or until salmon easily flakes with a fork.

Nutritional Counter Per Serving:

Calories 344, Carbs 3.4g, Protein 29.4g, Fat 23g, Cholesterol 83mg, Sodium 560mg, Fiber 0.7g

Romantic Shrimp Scampi

Homemade flavorful scampi for a romantic dinner.

Serves: 2

Preparation: 20 minutes

Total Time: 35 minutes

Ingredients:

30 medium shrimp, peeled, deveined

2 tablespoons butter, melted

2 tablespoons olive oil

2 garlic cloves, minced

1/2 teaspoon of kosher salt

1/4 teaspoon of ground black pepper

Directions:

1. Preheat the oven to 350°F.

2. Add olive oil, butter, garlic, salt and pepper to a bowl. Add the shrimp and toss then set aside for about 10 minutes.

3. Bake shrimp on sheet pan for about 15 minutes, or until cooked through.

Nutritional Counter Per Serving:

Calories 343, Carbs 1.2g, Protein 24.6g, Fat 26.4g, Cholesterol 259mg, Sodium 825mg, Fiber 0.1g

Weeknight Tilapia

Serves: 2

Preparation: 10 minutes

Total Time: 30 minutes

Ingredients:

2 tilapia fillets

1 tablespoon capers, drained

3 tablespoons sun-dried tomatoes packed in oil, drained, chopped

2 tablespoons kalamata olives, pitted, chopped

1 tablespoon lemon juice

1 tablespoon oil from the jar of sun-dried tomatoes

Directions:

1. Preheat your oven to 375°F.

2. In a small bowl, combine and stir together capers, tomatoes and olives. Set aside.

3. Place tilapia in a rimmed sheet pan then drizzle with lemon juice and oil (from the tomato jar).

4. Bake for 10-15 minutes, or until fish flakes easily with a fork.

5. Remove fish from oven and serve, topped with tomato mixture

Nutritional Counter Per Serving:

Calories 184, Carbs 5.4g, Protein 24.2g, Fat 7.2g, Cholesterol 41.0mg, Sodium 463mg, Fiber 1.1g

END

Thank you for reading my book. If you enjoyed it, won't you please take a moment to leave me a review at your favorite retailer? It means a lot to me.

Thanks!

Allison Barnes